River Rescue

by Peter Millett

illustrated by Emmanuel Cerisier

CAMBRIDGE
UNIVERSITY PRESS

UCL
Institute of Education

CHAPTER ONE

It was Saturday morning. Kamon Pattama was tired. Last week's school exams had been the hardest of his life. His father had promised to take him kayaking as a treat.

After breakfast, Mr Pattama, Kamon's father, checked the weather report on his phone. 'Oh, I see there's some bad weather coming later today.'

'Will we still be able to go kayaking?' Kamon asked.

'Perhaps we should go now, while it still looks fine,' said his father.

'Cool, I'm up for that,' Kamon beamed. He picked up his new drone. 'And maybe I could fly my drone after?'

'I'll think about it, but not if the weather turns bad.
I don't want to get wet watching you fly a drone around,'
his dad laughed.

'No problem,' Kamon said.

On their way to the river, it started to rain heavily
and thunder clouds rumbled above their heads.

Mr Pattama looked puzzled. 'The weather forecast
must have been completely wrong,' he said.
'Look - it's raining already.'

Kamon peered out of the car window.

'Maybe it's just a brief shower?' he said, hopefully.

Mr Pattama scanned the horizon. 'I don't think so.'

CHAPTER TWO

When they reached the river, the rain began
to fall even stronger and heavier. They parked close
to the dirt bank so that they could unload the kayaks,
ready to take them into the water.

Mr Pattama looked out at the heavy rain.
'I'm sorry, Kamon,' he said. 'This weather is
bad news for kayaking. Maybe we should leave it
until another day. Hopefully then the weather
forecasters will get it right.'

Suddenly, a great wall of water surged
down the river, smashing through the undergrowth,
sending rocks flying left and right.

'Look out!' Mr Pattama shouted, hitting
the accelerator to back the car away from the river.

'What's happening?' Kamon asked, anxiously.

'It's a flash flood!' his father cried. 'There must have been a land slip higher up the river.'

The water swept over the river banks, almost dragging Mr Pattama's car from where they had parked.

'This is crazy,' Kamon said. 'It took hardly any time at all to get to this. It's lucky we were not out there on the river. I'd hate to think what might have happened to us.'

He fell quiet and watched the dangerous waters thunder past him.

'Help! Help!' screamed two faint voices in the distance.

Mr Pattama turned round and looked up the river. 'Oh no! Look, Kamon. I think those boys are in serious trouble,' he cried.

Suddenly, a tall man banged on the car window.
He pointed to where Kamon had seen the two boys.

'HELP! I need you to help me! Please!
My sons are trapped out there in the middle of the river.'

A moment later, two kayaks slammed into the dirt bank just in front of them.

Mr Pattama opened his door and leapt out of the car.

'Shall we call the police?' asked Kamon.

'No,' said his father. 'There's not enough time. We must rescue them right now or they will be washed away down the river!'

CHAPTER THREE

Mr Pattama ran to the edge of the swelling river. Kamon followed.

'How can we reach them out there?' he cried.

His father shook his head.

'If we try and paddle out to them, we could drown,' he said. 'Then we are no help to anybody.'

'They need lifejackets,' said Kamon, 'to help save them from drowning.'

'How can we get lifejackets to them?' the boys' father asked. 'That's impossible without going into the water.'

Kamon ran back to the car. He had an idea that might just work. 'We have two lifejackets … I think I can fly them out to them,' he said.

'What?' the boys' father said. 'But how will you do that?'

'I can hook some rope under my drone and fly it out to them,' said Kamon. 'The rope can drag the lifejackets across the water to them.'

'Hey, that might just work,' said Mr Pattama. 'And maybe we can use the rope to pull the boys back as well.'

Kamon and his father looked for some long rope in the back of their car, but they couldn't find any.

'How about we use the ropes that are tying the kayaks to the roof?' said Kamon.

'Okay. But are you sure your drone is strong enough to carry this type of rope?' Mr Pattama asked.

'I don't know,' said Kamon. He untied the kayaks, lifted them down to the ground and unwound the long rope from the roof rack. 'I guess we're about to find out!'

Kamon hooked the rope under the drone.
Then he let it fly up into the air.

It struggled to fly in a straight line
with the weight of the long rope dragging
underneath it.

The drone had only been in the air for
a few seconds when a red light began
to flash on its controls.

Kamon's face dropped.

'What's that warning light for?' asked his dad.

'Oh no!' Kamon said. 'The battery is
running low. 'I forgot to charge it before
we left home.'

'What can we do?' asked the boys' father.

'Just keep flying it,' Mr Pattama said.
'Kamon's idea is the best chance
we have.'

CHAPTER FOUR

Slowly, the drone hovered its way
across the river towards the stranded boys.
The rope dangled just above the swirling currents.

'I hope the drone can make it before
the power runs out,' said Kamon.

The drone reached the rock where
the two boys were stranded.

'Unhook the rope!' Mr Pattama yelled out,
as the drone hovered above them.

The eldest boy stood up and tried to reach
the rope but he couldn't do it.
The battery warning level light began to flash faster.

'Come on, grab it,' Kamon breathed.

The younger brother stood up and reached out as far as he could. He could just reach the rope. He grasped it and managed to free it without crashing the drone.

The drone jolted skywards, suddenly free from the weight of the rope.

'Pull the rope towards you, as fast as you can,' the boys' father called out.

The boys pulled the rope towards them. The next sixty seconds felt like an hour, as the life jackets slowly slipped across the surface of the water and were dragged up onto the rock.

The boys pulled the life jackets down over their shoulders and fastened them.

18

'Now, I need you to be very brave
and get into the water!' Mr Pattama cried out to them.

CHAPTER FIVE

With its power almost completely gone, Kamon flew the drone back towards the river bank.

It landed next to him, just seconds before the motor cut out.

Mr Pattama and the boys' father wrapped the tail end of the rope around their waists.

'Okay boys, hold onto the rope tightly,' Mr Pattama called to them. 'Jump out as far as you can and we will drag you to safety.'

The boys gripped the rope hard and leapt into the surging waters.

The two men grunted and pulled as hard as they could.

Kamon turned the drone off.
Then he rushed over and joined in,
pulling the rope with all his might.

The boys hung on tightly
as the cold, muddy water smashed
into their faces.

Slowly but surely, they were
pulled back towards dry land.

'Our river rescue is working!'
Kamon cheered.

A few minutes later,
the exhausted boys crawled up
onto the slippery bank,
safe from the freezing waters.

Mr Pattama, Kamon
and the boys' father bent over,
panting hard as they finally
let go of the rope.

The two boys hugged their father and slipped off the lifejackets.

Kamon picked up his drone and smiled.

'Sorry, Dad,' he said. 'I guess you did end up getting wet watching me fly my drone around, after all!'

Mr Pattama hugged his son. 'Don't worry about that, Kamon,' he grinned. 'Today, I was very happy to do it.'

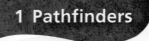

River Rescue Peter Millett

Teaching notes written by Sue Bodman and Glen Franklin

Using this book

Content/theme/subject

This exciting story follows Kamon and his father as they attempt to rescue two young boys stranded when a flash flood hits the river. Kamon's quick thinking saves the day. The story offers opportunities to consider multiple strands within the story line (for example, the interplay between the two different families) and causal effects, (the implication of Kamon deciding to take his drone to the river).

Language structure

- Contractions are used in speech for emphasis, including those easily confused with words without an apostrophe ('I'll' on p.3; 'we're' on p.13).
- The position of the reporting clause varies, either within or at the end of the dialogue, depending on the length of the sentence, and for authorial intent ('No,' said his father. 'There's not enough time.').

Book structure/visual features

- Short chapters provide breaks at key points in the story: 'cliff-hangers'.
- Paragraphing supports reading comprehension, for example by delineating events as they occur (p.13).

Vocabulary and comprehension

- Subject-specific vocabulary is used ('kayak', 'drone', 'life jackets', 'flash flood') and children will need to understand these terms as central to the plot.
- Character action is implied, such as how the two boys became stranded.

Curriculum links

Science – This book provides an example of how flash floods can build quickly and cause devastation. Use the Internet to investigate other flood disasters and explore what can be done to protect against them.

Maths – Write co-ordinates to map a path for the drone to reach the island and back to the river bank.

Learning outcomes

Children can:

- recall the main episodes, ideas and events of the story, when reading the same text over more than one lesson
- use morphology-based strategies to recall the meaning of words new to them
- listen to how their reading sounds, and monitor for effective oral delivery of their reading.

Planning for guided reading *River Rescue*

Lesson One Reading written speech orally and with expression to support comprehension.

Give a copy of the book to each child. Tell them the title and ask them to read the blurb and the first chapter (pages 2-3) quietly to themselves. Ask them to make note of any new vocabulary they do not understand to discuss with the whole group. Ask the children to tell you about the characters and setting. Discuss the genre (adventure story) and ask them to identify features that indicate this (style of illustrations, the weather warning). Notice how the chapter ends with 'I don't think so', indicating Kamon's father concern. Establish the meaning